INFOMOJIS

OCEAN LIFE

WAYLAND
www.waylandbooks.co.uk

First published in Great Britain
in 2018 by Wayland
Copyright © Hodder and Stoughton, 2018
All rights reserved

Executive editor: Adrian Cole
Produced by Tall Tree Ltd
Editor: Jon Richards
Designer: Ed Simkins

ISBN: 978 1 5263 0703 3

Wayland
An imprint of Hachette Children's Group
Part of Hodder and Stoughton
Carmelite House
50 Victoria Embankment
London EC4Y 0DZ

An Hachette UK Company
www.hachette.co.uk
www.hachettechildrens.co.uk

Printed and bound in China

LIVING IN THE SEA

It's the biggest habitat on the planet and it's got a range of wildlife to match. From the dark ocean depths to the sunlit waters of the surface, life in the ocean comes in a huge range of species, shapes and sizes, from tiny microscopic plants that drift on the ocean's currents to enormous whales.

Water world
You are probably sitting in a nice dry room, but did you know that more than 70 per cent of Earth's surface is covered by seas and oceans – better pack a swim suit!

Sail

Swimming shapes

Scales

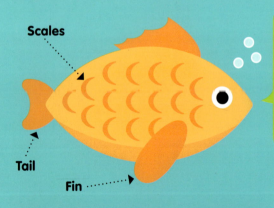

Tail

Fin

We **fish** have sleek, scale-covered bodies to move easily through the water. We use our tails and fins to push us along and steer us.

The **sailfish** is the speed king of ocean life, and can swim at up to 110 kilometres per hour.

Millions of years ago, a group of us **mammals** decided to move back to the sea. Legs and feet evolved into tails and flukes, and arms and hands became flippers.

Flipper

Ocean birds, like us **penguins**, have specially shaped wings that act like flippers as we zoom about under water.

We may be the smallest life in the ocean, but without us, nothing would exist in the water. As **phytoplankton**, we turn the Sun's energy into food that other living things depend on.

Exploring the deep
Conditions beneath the waves aren't good for us humans – we can't breathe underwater, the light fades quickly, and, before long, the pressure becomes so great that it could squash us flat. As a result, we know very little about life beneath the surface.

Q: How can we swim underwater?

A: Well you could take a VERY deep breath, or you could use something I developed. My name is Jacques Cousteau and in the 1940s I developed the aqua-lung, or **s**elf-**c**ontained **u**nderwater **b**reathing **a**pparatus (**SCUBA**).

Fluke

JACQUES COUSTEAU

SCUBA gear contains:

A regulator or demand valve to supply air into the mouth

A tank containing gasses to breathe

5

PLANTS AND ALGAE

If you thought ocean plants were dull and boring then you need to think again. Some of them are the smallest organisms in the seas, and without them, we wouldn't exist at all!

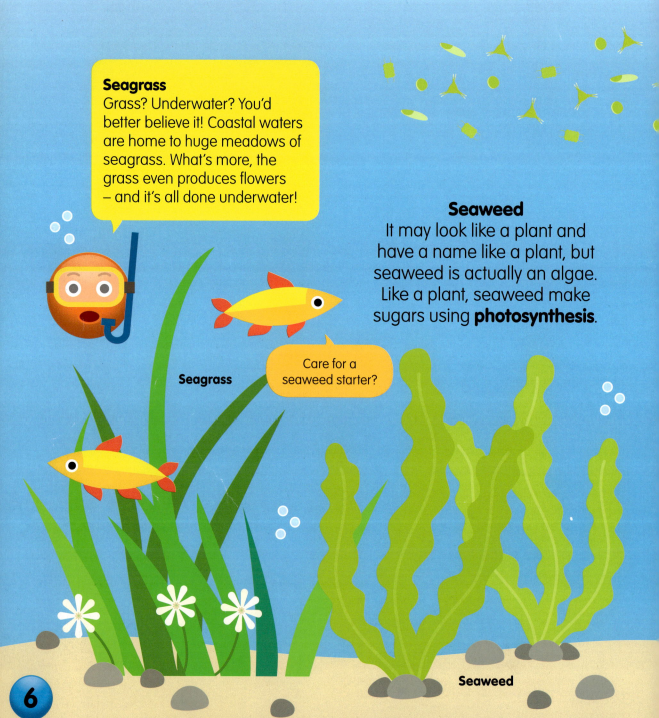

Seagrass
Grass? Underwater? You'd better believe it! Coastal waters are home to huge meadows of seagrass. What's more, the grass even produces flowers – and it's all done underwater!

Seaweed
It may look like a plant and have a name like a plant, but seaweed is actually an algae. Like a plant, seaweed make sugars using **photosynthesis**.

Care for a seaweed starter?

Seagrass

Seaweed

Phytoplankton
Hey! We're over here! We're small but there are lots of us and I do mean LOTS! There are about 5,000 species of phytoplankton living in the seas and they come in lots of different shapes and sizes.

Phytoplankton are usually too small to be seen with the naked eye, but when conditions are right they can gather together in huge blooms that are so big they can be seen from space!

Phytoplankton are tiny plants. They absorb minerals that well up from the ocean depths and use sunlight to produce sugars in a process called photosynthesis. As a result, they form the basis of the ocean food chain and play a key role in keeping life in the ocean alive.

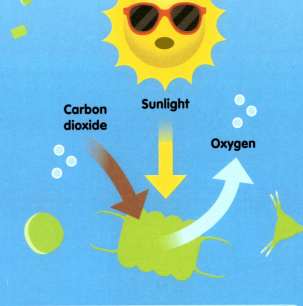

Carbon dioxide

Sunlight

Oxygen

Some calculations show that marine phytoplankton may produce up to 85 per cent of the world's oxygen.

Sargassum is a free-floating seaweed. In 2015, so much washed up on Caribbean beaches that the gases released when it rotted produced stinking smells and could rust metals and damage property.

Seaweeds like sargassum float around freely, but most use a root-like holdfast to fix themselves firmly to the seabed.

BEACHES AND SHORE LIFE

Living on beaches is no place for the faint-hearted. When you're not battered by waves, you're left exposed when the water pulls back, ready for some pesky predator to come and pick you off for lunch!

These long legs come in handy for us **wading birds** as we walk through the shallow water looking for a tasty snack. Now, have you seen a lugworm anywhere?

Time and tide
Twice a day, seawater moves up and down the shoreline. This regular movement is called the tide and it is caused by the gravitational attraction of the Sun and the Moon on Earth's oceans.

High tide – highest water mark, covering the shoreline.

Low tide – lowest water mark, exposing the shoreline.

Long slim bill perfect for getting buried worms.

Worm casts

Long legs keep the bird's body out of the water.

Buried worms
Hey watch where you're stepping! When the tide is out, we lugworms hide in our holes, waiting for the water to return. You can see the worm casts we leave behind on the surface – that's worm poo to you!

Intertidal zone

The area between high and low tide is called the intertidal zone.

Peek-a-boo!

Organisms living at the top of the intertidal zone spend more time out of the water than in it, so they risk drying out. To stop this, they can either find shelter or pull themselves into their body or a shell. Organisms living at the bottom of this zone have to cope with the energy of the waves, and they usually have ways of fixing themselves firmly to the floor.

Mini water world

When the tide goes out, small puddles of water are trapped in rock pools, providing mini oases for water life.

If I fancy a shellfish to eat, I just clamp it in my powerful arms, pull the shells apart and then slip my stomach through the crack and digest the yummy goodies inside.

This is the perfect spot to hide out from any pesky seabirds and maybe find something good to eat.

Put your hands in the air! **Sea anemones** wave tentacles in the water to catch tiny food particles.

Starfish

Sea anemone

Crab

With more than 100 rows of teeth, we **limpets** have one tough bite. These teeth are handy when it comes to scraping algae off rocks.

Limpet

COASTAL WATERS

With sunlit waters and plenty of nutrients welling up from the ocean deep, coastal waters are the perfect home for a whole host of amazing plants and animals.

Continental shelf
The continental shelf surrounds Earth's major landmasses, and stretches about 70 km from the shore. The waters here are quite shallow and less than 200 metres deep, which means there's plenty of sunlight for sea plants to produce energy and feed the rest of the ocean food chain.

Continental shelf

Kelp forests
Anchored to the sea floor, huge forests of kelp teem with a wide range of ocean life.

Kelp is a type of marine algae, like seaweed.

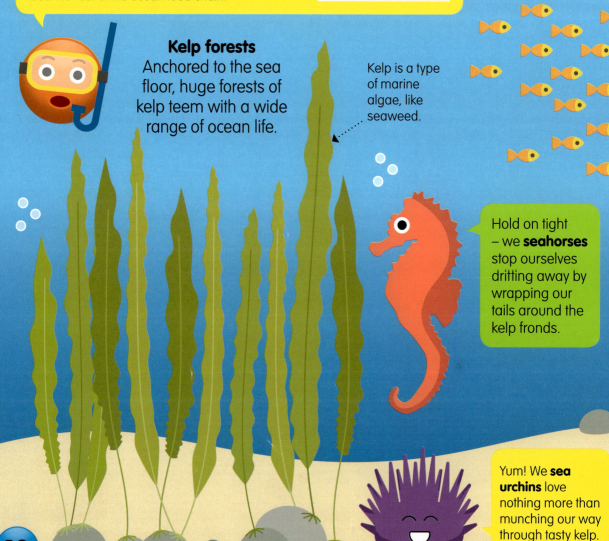

Hold on tight – we **seahorses** stop ourselves dritting away by wrapping our tails around the kelp fronds.

Yum! We **sea urchins** love nothing more than munching our way through tasty kelp.

Fishing birds
Loads of fish mean loads of birds. And they don't get much better at fishing than us pelicans. With a long beak and an expandable throat pouch, we can scoop fish right out of the water.

Cleaning time
Feel like getting clean? Then pay me a visit. I'm a **cleaner wrasse**, and I can pick off any stray scales and parasites from some fish.

Moo?

Underwater grazers
What eats sea grass? **Sea cows** of course! Also known as **manatees** and **dugongs**, these large mammals take a deep breath and slip beneath the waves. They munch their way through clumps of seagrass, feeding at depths of up to 40 metres. Dugongs can be found in the western Pacific and Indian Oceans, while manatees are found in the Caribbean Sea, Amazon river and the coasts and rivers of West Africa.

Coastal fish
Why are **flatfish** perfectly adapted to living on the sea floor – because they're flat! With both eyes on one side of their body, they can lie flat against the mud (and sometimes in it!), hiding from predators or waiting to snatch something to eat.

CORAL REEFS

Prepare yourself for the hustle and bustle of the ocean's busiest ecosystem. They are some of the largest natural structures on the planet, but coral reefs are built by some of the tiniest animals known.

Coral reefs cover just 0.1 per cent of the ocean, but they are home to at least 25 per cent of all marine species.

Atoll formation

1. A volcanic island stops erupting and becomes extinct.

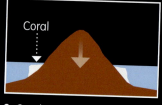

Coral

2. Coral growth forms a ring around the island, which starts to subside.

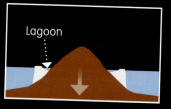

Lagoon

3. The reef grows in size as the island continues to sink, forming a lagoon.

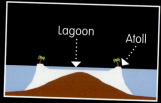

Lagoon   Atoll

4. The island disappears below the sea, leaving an atoll surrounding a lagoon.

Powerful polyps
We may be tiny, but we're certainly mighty. I measure less than 3 mm across, but I can build a tough rocky case around my body to protect myself. Then, when I die, another polyp does the same on top of my rocky skeleton, building up layer after layer of coral, until you have a huge reef.

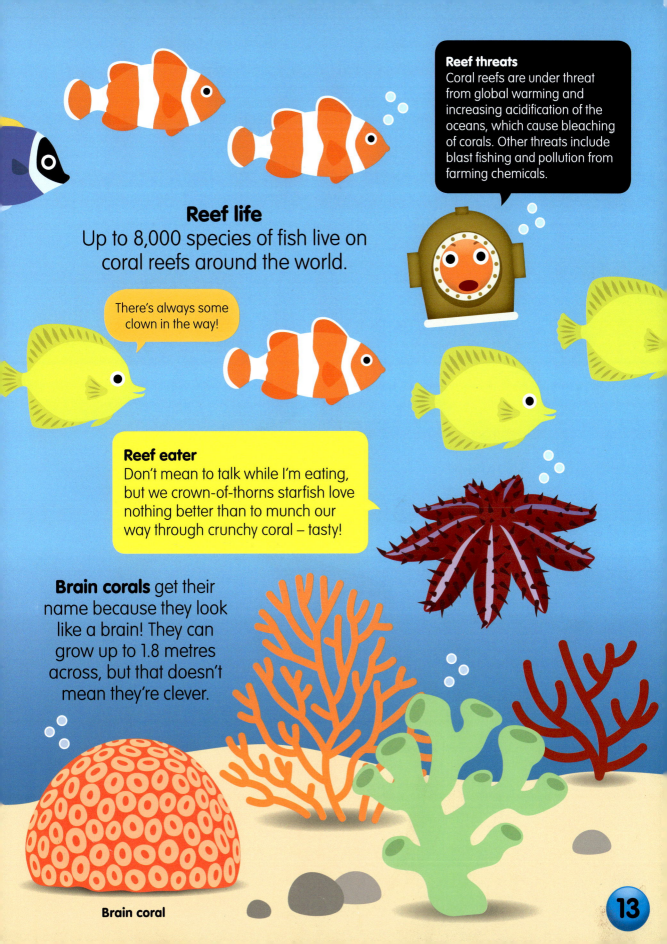

Reef life
Up to 8,000 species of fish live on coral reefs around the world.

There's always some clown in the way!

Reef eater
Don't mean to talk while I'm eating, but we crown-of-thorns starfish love nothing better than to munch our way through crunchy coral – tasty!

Brain corals get their name because they look like a brain! They can grow up to 1.8 metres across, but that doesn't mean they're clever.

Brain coral

OPEN OCEAN

They make up most of the world's oceans, but these areas do not support much in the way of ocean life because they are lacking in nutrients. So when predators do find something to eat, they make the most of it.

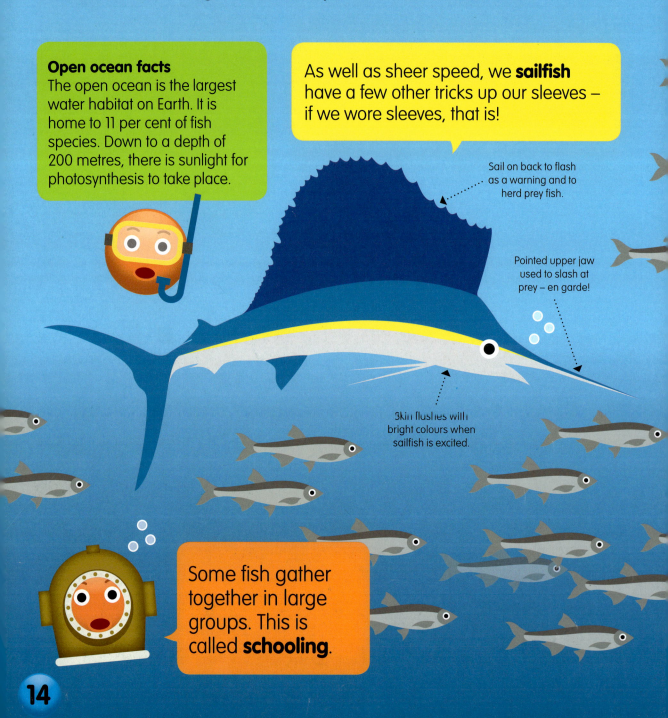

Open ocean facts
The open ocean is the largest water habitat on Earth. It is home to 11 per cent of fish species. Down to a depth of 200 metres, there is sunlight for photosynthesis to take place.

As well as sheer speed, we **sailfish** have a few other tricks up our sleeves – if we wore sleeves, that is!

Sail on back to flash as a warning and to herd prey fish.

Pointed upper jaw used to slash at prey – en garde!

Skin flushes with bright colours when sailfish is excited.

Some fish gather together in large groups. This is called **schooling**.

Dive bombers

Well it would be a shame to waste all these fish! So **gannets** dive from 30 metres or more, reaching about 100 kph to catch these tasty treats underwater.

Schooling helps us to forage for food.

We join together in schools to protect ourselves from hunters.

Gannet

Dolphin

Schooling fact
Scientists estimate that herring can form super schools measuring 5 cubic km and containing about three billion fish.

Schooling helps us to find mates and reproduce.

School hunters
Some species of **dolphin** have been recorded herding schools of fish into lines of waiting dolphins who pick off the oncoming fish. When schools are big enough, dolphins can gather in groups of more than 15,000 to join in the feast.

In a school, we can swim more efficiently.

Other hunters join in the feast, including **orcas**, who use their huge tails to swat and stun the schooling fish.

Orca

OCEAN DEPTHS

Below 200 metres, the sunlight fades and things turn black. Living down in these dark depths are some of the strangest creatures on the planet.

The surface of Mars has been mapped in more detail than the ocean floor.

Dragonfish

Living lights

Many deep-sea creatures produce lights. This is called bioluminescence.

Anglerfish

Marine snow
Don't think you want to make a snowman out of this stuff! Falling from the upper levels of the ocean is a shower of bits and pieces of organic matter. Scientists call this yucky stuff marine snow and it's a vital source of food for deep-sea creatures.

Be careful – not everything is what it seems to be! **Dragonfish** and **anglerfish** use lures – lights on the ends of barbels – to attract prey towards their sharp, teeth-filled jaws.

'Now you see me, now you don't' – many creatures, like us **firefly squid** use lights to hide from predators lurking below.

Firefly squid

Super-hot vents

With temperatures of more than 460 degrees Celsius, no sunlight and crushing pressures, conditions around hydrothermal vents are not the most comfortable on the planet. But even here, living things have found a way to survive.

Tube worms

Huge 17-centimetre long **amphipods**, like enormous shrimps, are specially adapted to life in the depths.

Deepsea Challenger

Only three people have ever journeyed to the bottom of Challenger Deep.

A huge type of sea cucumber called a **holothurian**.

Giant amoebas called **xenophyophores** are some of the largest cells on the planet.

Down to the depths

When I reached the bottom of the ocean floor in March 2012 in my submersible *Deepsea Challenger*, there wasn't much to see at first, but all sorts of strange creatures soon appeared.

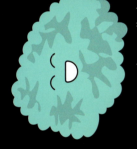

JAMES CAMERON

The average depth of the oceans is 3,688 metres. Challenger Deep (the deepest part of Earth's Oceans) is 10,898–10,916 metres below the surface. Down here, the weight of the water above increases the pressure so that it is about 1,100 times the pressure at sea level.

17

POLAR WATERS

Brrrrrrr! Make sure you wrap up warm as we plunge into the icy waters that are found around our planet's poles. The seas here may be inhospitable, but they can still teem with all sorts of living things.

I'm not swimming if they're in there!

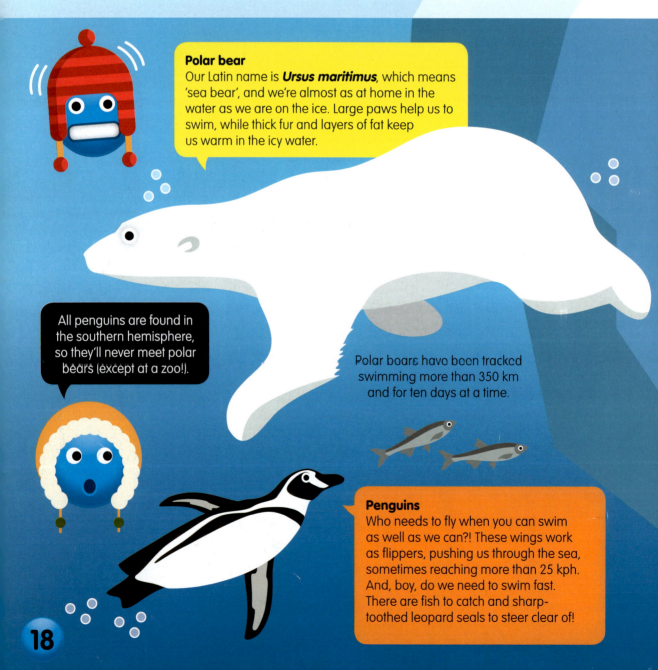

Polar bear
Our Latin name is *Ursus maritimus*, which means 'sea bear', and we're almost as at home in the water as we are on the ice. Large paws help us to swim, while thick fur and layers of fat keep us warm in the icy water.

All penguins are found in the southern hemisphere, so they'll never meet polar bears (except at a zoo!).

Polar bears have been tracked swimming more than 350 km and for ten days at a time.

Penguins
Who needs to fly when you can swim as well as we can?! These wings work as flippers, pushing us through the sea, sometimes reaching more than 25 kph. And, boy, do we need to swim fast. There are fish to catch and sharp-toothed leopard seals to steer clear of!

Q: What do you get if you cross a whale with a unicorn?

A: A narwhal!

tusk

Narwhal's are medium-sized whales and we males have one long canine tooth that sticks out like a tusk. This special tooth is filled with sense endings and we use it to communicate and catch prey.

Narwhal

Leopard seal

Icefish
Cold water? No problem? Not when you have antifreeze for blood. An icefish has special chemicals in its blood that stop it from freezing in the icy water.

Underwater leopards
You'd better swim fast! With its razor-sharp teeth, a leopard seal will make short work of munching through a tasty penguin snack. They weigh more than half a tonne, but can still zoom through the water at more than 35 kph.

Icefish

GIANTS OF THE OCEAN

Living in the ocean is perfect for growing large. Surrounded and supported by water means that marine creatures can reach super-size.

Ocean sunfish
I may not look like the fastest fish in the ocean, but I'm the biggest. At least the biggest bony fish, that is! With our round bodies, we sunfish swim through warmer sea waters looking for tasty jellyfish, squid and small fish to eat.

Sunfish

Female ocean sunfish can release up to **300,000,000** eggs at one time.

Whale shark
We're big in size, like whales, and we filter tiny plankton out of the water, but that's where the similarity ends. We're actually fish and the biggest ever fish at that. We're also sharks and that means we don't have a bony skeleton, but one made from bendy cartilage.

Whale sharks grow to more than 12 metres long and weigh 21 tonnes.

Whale shark

Blue whale

If it's big you want, then you won't get much bigger than us. In fact, there's NEVER been an animal bigger than us. Blue whales grow to nearly 30 metres long and weigh more than a 150 tonnes.

Blue whales may be gigantic, but they eat tiny food, filtering microscopic **plankton** out of the water.

A blue whale will munch through **4 tonnes** of plankton every day.

Giant squid and octopuses

Legends talk about giant sea creatures who pulled sailors and even ships to their doom! Could they have been giant octopuses or giant squid? These huge creatures live in the deep ocean, where they hunt for fish and try to keep out of the way of sperm whales that hunt them.

Giant octopuses measure nearly 3.5 metres and weigh more than 70 kilograms.

Giant squid reach 13 metres long and weigh about 275 kg.

WEIRD AND WONDERFUL

We know so little about the underwater world. Every year scientists are discovering more and more species of living things, some of which can look pretty strange!

Clown frogfish
My body is covered in warty lumps and bumps, which help me to hide against coral. And my super-wide mouth lets me snap up prey as big as I am!

Clown frogfish

Sea cucumber
They might not look like much, but you don't want to get too close to sea cucumbers – especially if you plan on eating one! Many of them are highly toxic and a few have some 'special' defences to put off attackers. They squirt sticky tubules out of their bums to trap a predator while they get away – nice!

Tubules

Pardon me!

Manta rays can measure up to 3 metres across.

Flying rays
Why swim when you can fly? A ray's huge pectoral fins are like enormous wings and they flap them to move through the water. They can even leap out of the water!

At least my mum loves me!

Blobfish
If you think frogfish look ugly, then get a load of this! Blobfish live in the dark murky depths off the coast of Australia (probably so other fish can't see them) and they've been voted the world's ugliest animal – so it's official!

Blobfish

Red-lipped batfish
It may look like this fish is wearing lipstick, but these red lips may play an important part in getting a mate. Kissy, kissy!

Give us a kiss!

Batfish use their specially adapted pectoral fins to 'walk' along the seabed

Red-lipped batfish

23

PREDATORS AND PREY

Living in the ocean is about eating and being eaten (or rather NOT being eaten). Marine animals have many clever ways of tracking and catching food, and some have more ingenious ways of avoiding being eaten.

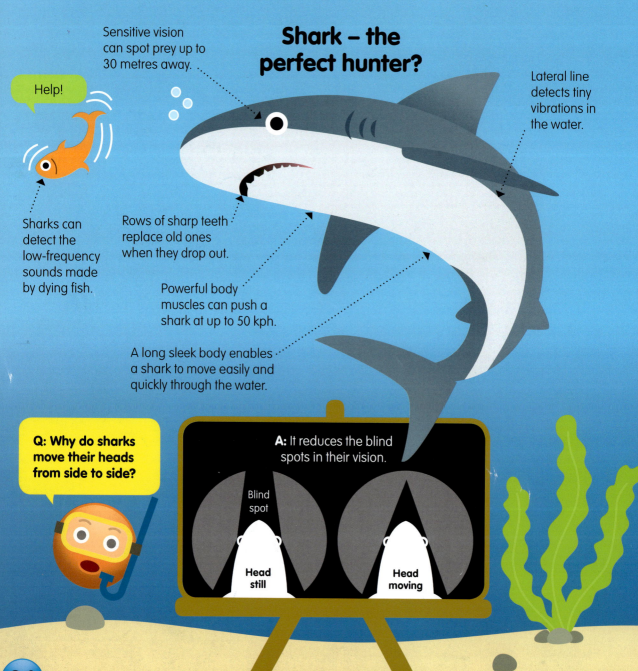

Shark – the perfect hunter?

Sensitive vision can spot prey up to 30 metres away.

Lateral line detects tiny vibrations in the water.

Help!

Sharks can detect the low-frequency sounds made by dying fish.

Rows of sharp teeth replace old ones when they drop out.

Powerful body muscles can push a shark at up to 50 kph.

A long sleek body enables a shark to move easily and quickly through the water.

Q: Why do sharks move their heads from side to side?

A: It reduces the blind spots in their vision.

Blind spot

Head still

Head moving

Sting in the tail
The **Portuguese man o'war** has long tentacles with venomous stings, which they use to kill small fish to eat.

We swim slowly, but us **pufferfish** have a special trick if threatened. Our super-stretchy stomachs mean we can puff up to form a huge ball. And some of us have sharp spikes just to make ourselves a little harder-to-eat.

But that's not all! Pufferfish contain a deadly toxin in their bodies – enough to kill 30 adult humans.

Ink
Squid and octopuses squirt out dark ink when threatened to confuse the predator ... Hey! Where did they go?

Speed machines
Tuna are some of the fastest fish in the ocean, tearing through the water at up to 75 kph as they hunt down prey or escape a hungry predator.

Tuna

OCEAN TRAVELLERS

The seas and oceans cover more than 70 per cent of Earth's surface. They are connected with each other, making them perfect highways for travelling around the planet.

Q: Why do sea creatures migrate?

A: Food! As resources in one region decrease, they increase in others, so animals move to where there's enough to eat.

A: Have babies! Giving birth and raising young takes plenty of energy, and sea creatures need conditions that are good for reproduction.

- - - **Northern elephant seals** – up to 21,000 km between California and Alaska

- - - **Pacific Bluefin tuna** – 8,000 km between Sea of Japan and California

- - - **Leatherback turtle** – 20,500 km between Indonesia and west coast of USA

- - - **Grey whales** – 16,000 km between Mexico and Alaska

- - - **Humpback whales** – 16,500 km between Costa Rica and Antarctica

- - - **European eel** – European freshwater and Sargasso Sea

ALASKA

MEXICO

SOUTH AMERICA

Terrific travellers
If it's long distance you're after, then you can't travel much further than these magnificent migrators.

OCEANS IN TROUBLE

Even though the vast oceans are so big and cover so much of the planet, our actions have had a damaging effect on this enormous ecosystem and the animals and plants living there.

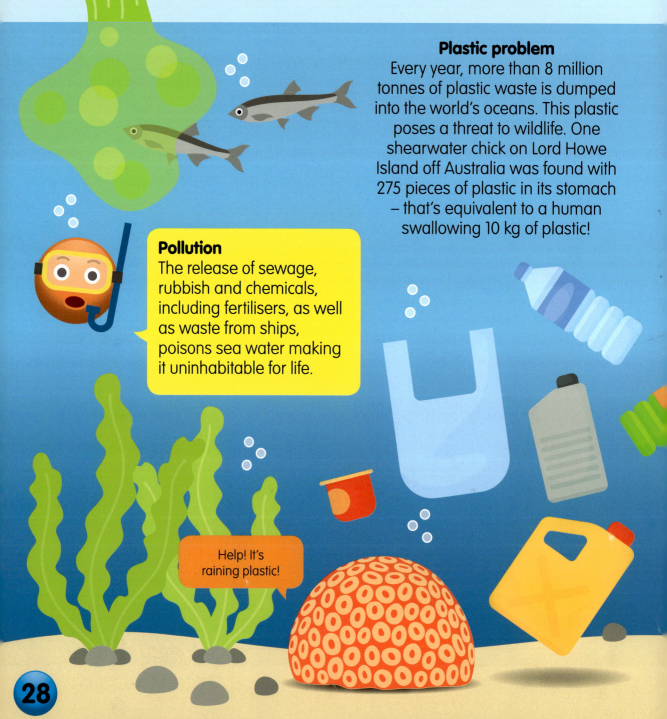

Plastic problem

Every year, more than 8 million tonnes of plastic waste is dumped into the world's oceans. This plastic poses a threat to wildlife. One shearwater chick on Lord Howe Island off Australia was found with 275 pieces of plastic in its stomach – that's equivalent to a human swallowing 10 kg of plastic!

Pollution

The release of sewage, rubbish and chemicals, including fertilisers, as well as waste from ships, poisons sea water making it uninhabitable for life.

Help! It's raining plastic!

Global warming
Warming temperatures lead to rising sea levels, an increase in the acid levels in water and the destruction of many marine habitats.

Overfishing
Over the years, people have taken too many fish out of the seas, leading to a huge reduction in fish stocks, which cannot replace themselves. According to the WWF, about 90 per cent of the world's fisheries have been fully exploited or overfished.

Protecting and preserving
Governments around the world are dedicating parts of the ocean and turning them into Marine Protected Areas where fishing is controlled and pollution restricted. But they make up less than 4 per cent of Earth's oceans.

Whaling
Whales have been hunted for thousands of years, but the huge numbers killed in the 19th and 20th centuries saw many species almost disappear. Despite a huge reduction in whaling today, estimates are that some whale populations are less than 10 per cent of their peak.

GLOSSARY

ACIDIFICATION
To increase the amount of acid levels in a substance. Increased levels of acid can have harmful effects on plants and animals living in water.

ALGAE
A type of living thing that grows on damp surfaces or in water and uses photosynthesis to get energy from sunlight.

ANTIFREEZE
A substance that stops liquids from freezing solid.

ATOLL
A ring-shaped coral reef that surrounds an island and a lagoon.

BARBELS
Long, thin spines that hang from the jaws and heads of some fish.

BIOLUMINESCENCE
The production of light by living things including some insects, such as fireflies, and fish, such as anglerfish.

BLAST FISHING
Using explosives to stun and kill fish. Blast fishing also harms other wildlife and can cause huge amounts of damage to coral reefs.

BLIND SPOT
An area where vision is obscured or where you can't see anything at all.

CARTILAGE
A strong but bendy body tissue that makes up your ears and nose and the skeletons of cartilaginous fish, such as sharks and rays.

CONTINENTAL SHELF
An area surrounding the world's continents where the waters are shallow.

CORAL POLYPS
Tiny marine animals, some of which make hard outer cases that build up over time to form coral reefs.

ECOSYSTEM
The plants and animals that live in a particular area and how they interact with the environment.

FERTILISERS
A substance that is spread over farmland to improve the growth and output of crops.

FLUKES
The two flat lobes on the tail of a whale.

FOOD CHAIN
The relationship between different living things where one living thing feeds on the next one to it in the chain.

GLOBAL WARMING
The increase in the world's temperature.

HABITAT
The natural environment in which a plant or animal lives.

HOLDFAST
The root-like structure that fixes seaweed to the sea floor.

HYDROTHERMAL VENT
A crack in the sea floor through which super-hot water wells up. The water has been heated by volcanic processes below the surface.

INTERTIDAL ZONE
The area of the shoreline between high tide and low tide.

LAGOON
A calm area of sea that is surrounded by a reef or land.

LATERAL LINE
A line of sensitive organs that runs along the sides of fish. It detects vibrations and pressure changes in the water.

LURE
An object or part of a body that is used to attract prey towards a predator or trap.

MAMMAL
A type of animal that usually gives birth to live young and produces milk to feed its young.

MIGRATE
To move from one place to another. Animals migrate in search of food and water or to find a suitable place to give birth and raise young.

PARASITE
A small plant or animal that lives in or on another living thing and gets food from it.

PECTORAL FINS
Fins that grow out of the chest of a fish or marine mammal.

PHOTOSYNTHESIS
The process in which energy from the Sun is converted into sugars.

PLANKTON
Tiny plants and animals that live in water.

REPRODUCE
When plants and animals produce young.

SCHOOL
The name given to a group of fish.

SPECIES
Plants and animals that have the same characteristics and can reproduce with each other to produce fertile young.

INDEX